On Not Being Observed

Dave Morgan is a writer, community educator and arts organiser in the North-West of England, who was brought up in the Potteries. He co-founded the performance poetry organisation Write Out Loud and curates events for Live from Worktown, the Bolton-based arts collective. Dave has had a lifelong interest in China and the Far East, and a selection of work from his previous collection, *Chuang Tse's Caterpillar*, has recently been translated into Tamil for South Asian journal *Thalam Quarterly*. He tries to balance his personal passions for nature and quiet reflection with a recurring mission to help change people's lives for the better and drink in good company.

By the author

China: An Integrated Study *

Chuang Tse's Caterpillar

On Not Being Observed

* Co-authored with Arthur Cotterell
and published by George G. Harrap & Co Ltd

DAVE MORGAN

On Not Being Observed

Flapjack Press

flapjackpress.co.uk

Exploring the synergy between performance and the page

Published in 2024 by Flapjack Press
Salford, Gtr Manchester

⊕ flapjackpress.co.uk · **f** Flapjack Press
𝕏 flapjackpress · ▶ flapjackpress2520

ISBN 978-1-7396231-3-5

Printed by Imprint Digital
Exeter, Devon
⊕ digital.imprint.co.uk

A UNESCO City
of Literature

northern
fiction
alliance

To my memory, you stalwart,
if somewhat unreliable, fellow traveller.
Here's to you while we're still in touch.

Contents

Foreword

There is much to enjoy in this collection. Dave Morgan has an eye for detail – and for the absurd. There is a sense of looking back – over seventy years – in poems that are as sharply focused as a series of high-definition photographs. Decades of life, friendships, and relationships in poems of good-humour, where even revisited regrets and longings find a form of acceptance. There are poems that will chime, in particular, with those who have experience of northern communities – and with those of 'a certain age'! Morgan's nostalgic approach never becomes maudlin or sentimental but will evoke your own recollections.

Warning: reading this collection will make you want to take the author out for a pint to draw out more of his stories.

Sarah Maclennan
Head of Creative Writing
Liverpool John Moores University
March 2024

Introduction

Poetry is a wonderful medium for autobiography. Generally it's concise and generally it punches above its weight. Poems may assume to be about things, events, ideas, observations, reflections. I propose that they are really only about one thing: the poet. The wonderful diversity and yet perverse synchronicity of poetry reflects both our uniqueness and our universal oneness. I submit that poetry is ultimately about the human condition and the condition of the poet creating it. I have undertaken no research or literary analysis to support this proposition. Goodbye my fantasy doctorate.

Dave Morgan
January 2024

On not being observed

Intoxicated
Just the moon for company
He toasts the heavens

Sitting alone with my memories,
I'd gladly exchange them for
A decent pint or a decent pee.
They're not taking me
Anywhere I want to be tonight.

They're a six-lane highway.
They're a pitch-black tunnel.
They're a mountain goat track.
They're an emergency flight path.
They're an ocean shipping lane.
They're a satellite trajectory.

Memory Lane.
It's a fucking cul-de-sac.

Childhood fruits

This is a banana.
Don't eat the skin.
Snap the end and peel it back.
Slice it sideways and place between
Two slices of bread and butter.
That way it does for Thursday's tea.

I know you don't like oranges.
They make a mess, they're sticky.
The cheap ones we buy are sometimes sour.
Peel it carefully,
Take off the bitter pith.
Slice into rounds and eat with lots of sugar.

It's a coconut silly.
Gloria's boyfriend won it at the wakes.
Isn't he clever?
It's come all the way from Africa.
Shake it and listen to the milk.
Now fetch a hammer and a nail.

These grapes?
No, you can't have one.
They're for your Aunty Nelly.
She's in hospital, she's not well.
A bunch of grapes will help her feel much better.
You're not ill, so keep your hands off.

Apples? Apples?
Yes, you can have an apple.
What do you mean can you have two?

There's more than just you in this house you know.
I never heard of such a thing.
Can I have two? I never did.

No, a pomegranate. Pom…ee…gran…it.
Yes, watch carefully.
A sharp knife will cut it in two.
Then take this pin and lift each seed.
Here's a tea towel.
Make sure you chew each one or you'll get appendicitis.

A pineapple. Our Billy bought it in the pub.
No, it's not from a tin,
This is how they look for real.
Let's cut it into rings and cubes,
And if it's not as nice as tinned
We'll put some sugar on it.

Keep your hands off that bowl of fruit.
They collected at your dad's works
As a mark of their respect.
It has to sit on the sideboard and be admired.
I wish they'd sent the money, fruit won't pay the rent.
You can have some after the funeral.

Sole man

He would never have been seen in trainers.
Any work boots he had were kept at work.
You can tell a man's standing by the state of his shoes.
He was an old-fashioned shoe fan.
With black polished Oxfords and brogues in tan,
He was a sole man, a leather sole man.

At a loose end and before a big event,
Or as part of his regular Sunday ritual,
He laid out his kit on last night's *Sentinel*
And polished and buffed to his heart's content.
Those black polished Oxfords and brogues in tan,
He was a sole man, a leather sole man.

They lined up in pairs, heels facing out,
Under the gleaming oakwood sideboard.
Caressed by Kiwi, cherished by Cherry Blossom,
Each pair waiting to be treated in turn.
The black polished Oxfords and the brogues in tan,
He was a proper shoe fan, a leather sole man.

He despaired at my winklepickers,
My crêpe-soled beetle crushers.
Damage your feet, man, make them sweat.
You can tell a man's standing by the state of his shoes.
With his black shiny Oxfords and brogues in tan,
He was an 'old-school' man, a leather sole fan.

He knew that shoes were a man's best friend
And treated each pair with deep respect.

They repaid him amply, lasting for years,
Until his feet complained and rejected them,
Those black leather Oxfords and brogues in tan.
He lost his soles man, his leather soles man.

His aching bones grew so misshapen,
The well-groomed footwear gathered dust.
How I struggled with my weasel words,
How he struggled with his silent hurt.
Those black polished Oxfords and brogues in tan,
They were his soles man, not my soles man.

Thirty years on I considered my shoes,
And the scent of new leather and cobblers' dye,
With a sense of wellbeing in restoring life
To my black leather Oxfords and my brogues in tan.
I became a sole man, a leather sole man.

Everyone avoids eye contact and disowns the man who dances on tables at the Catholic Club as if to say he's not with us. Okay, it's New Year's Eve and it's 'Singing in the Rain' time and the man who's never had a dancing lesson in his life thinks he's Gene Kelly and the table is full of half-filled glasses and one of its legs is wonky but not as wonky as his but just because he's the Chairman's brother-in-law they pretend it's not happening.

What's transformed him other than six pints of Guinness and a bottle of red wine? He's in a world of his own, he's in a film of his own, surrounded by a family who act as if it's normal until the table tilts just a little too far and a stentorian voice cuts through the orchestration to bring him to his senses to spoil his fantasy.

'Get down off there our David, people will think you're daft.' And by implication *we are too*.

Family-shaming reduces the fifty-year-old man who dances on tables to a five-year-old boy who has just thrown-up at the local Church Christmas Party after gorging himself on every forbidden sweet and treat.

'That's your trouble. You can't just enjoy yourself. You have to take things too far.'

What are you trying to tell me?

Your eyes, grey and vacant,
Follow me down High Streets
Returning my stare from each shop front.
From train windows I catch your furtive glance
Before returning to my book.
What are you trying to tell me?

I cast you aside many years ago,
I buried you and sang at your wake.
You have less hair than I remember,
But it's that moustache that gets me.
Why the moustache?
What are you trying to tell me?

A life of biblical proportions

In my seventieth year
I have abandoned nakedness in favour of winceyette,
Abstain for two days after every binge,
Exercise my smile muscles for sixty seconds before taking my statin,
Have brunch thus saving one meal a day,
Try to maintain Henry Miller's maxim 'Always merry and bright'
After a lifetime of whingeing.
My sexual habits have changed.
Let me say no more.
In winter I take five minutes in the hour to observe my bird feeders.
In summer, rain permitting, I wander my garden paths
Musing on passing time,
The arcing sun behind the trees,
The subtle passage of the shade.
I marvel at the fecundity of runner beans,
Question the paucity of peas.
Wonder where all the frogs have gone.
Planning, planning for next year.
No longer so focused on other people's needs,
I work at not feeling guilty.
I accept the past, neither rejecting nor denying it.
I try to keep engaged.
I try to avoid other old people but there are a lot of them about.
I have systems to remember where my car keys are,
To remember my grandkids' birthdays,
To remember to take damp clothes out of the washing machine.
So much to remember.
I don't know how I found time to hold down a job,
Drink excessively, stay out to unearthly hours and
Maintain a stable of mistresses.

Incontinence and impotence remind me a clock is ticking.
Vanity is pointless.
No longer the night owl I used to be,
I read late until my eyes droop.
Do I sleep better?
No but my dreams are enjoyable.
Cutting in and out at will
I wait for the day when dream and life are indistinguishable.

For what life is there...? *

Winter sun glinting
On tinned-up terraces.
Compulsory purchase.

The thief stole it all.
Happiness, memories, trust.
Just fading tokens.

On the wasteland,
Naked but for a tarnished bauble,
Last year's Christmas tree.

Playing in the ruins.
Homes flattened not by bombs
But by planners.

The last of the few
Behind barricades and banners.
Resistance futile.

Who's that cowering
Beneath that big black boot?
The woman in the street.

It may be hell today,
But if the bully has his way
It'll be murder tomorrow.

Laughing at *Shameless*,
Face to face with their worst fears
Behind locked doors.

Newspaper headlines,
Sex, Drugs, Migrants, Scroungers.
He only buys it for the racing.

Devolve the budgets,
Empower the people.
Look! A flying pig.

Community
Sustainability
Means… do it yourself.

Losing your will to live?
Don't worry, trust us, believe.
Tomorrow you *will* eat cake.

Hanging baskets?
Hanging tyrants.
That's community action.

* '…if not in community?' – W.H. Auden

Garam masala

Mr Johnson is walking the tarmacked ribs of Queens Park
With all its restored Victorian orderliness
When over the brow appear a phalanx of heavy-coated figures,
Arms swinging, maintaining an insistent pace,
Approaching in double-time.
His dog, Missie, wary of their resolution, takes a wide berth,
But as they bounce closer on garish Skechers
Johnson offers a cheery 'garam masala ladies.'
Liptrot has told him this means 'peace be with you' in Urdu.
He's been to Goa you know.
The leaders laugh and wish him a good morning,
Before marching their troops over the bridge
And back to their ruminating elders and puking infants,
Confident in the knowledge that a few pounds have been shed,
And pleased (Johnson is convinced) that at least one
Ageing Englishman is prepared to go that extra mile
In the interest of cross-cultural goodwill and understanding.

The behemoths meet
Trolley to trolley in the alcohol aisle
Before their wives track them down
And break them up.
Desperate Dans, raised on cow pie,
They used to say shelf-stacking was for the simple-minded
When shovelling ten ton a shift,
Black dust getting where the sun doesn't shine.
Now they'd resurrect their grandad's fighting clogs
To get twenty hours a week corralling trolleys
On the supermarket car park,
To see the missus supervising on the deli counter,
One eye fixed on the sell-by-date of quiche.

The Health Service is full of bureaucrats
Local Government is full of apparatchiks
The Civil Service is full of mandarins
The schools are full of whingers
The streets are full of spongers.
The only ones who can save us now
Are the City, the Hedge Funds, the drinks giants,
The tobacco corporations, the oil conglomerates,
The gambling empires, the pharmaceutical dynasties.
At times like this you get to know who your real friends are.

Over there a person dies before their time
Surrounded by blue- or green-clad acolytes, a proxy family
If lucky; or maybe quietly, unobserved, or at worst ignored.
Over here the sun seduces, lures us, calls us to play,
Allows us time to share and care for family
Unless they're in need; on the outside looking in
We thought we were invincible.
Somewhere innocence is lost, freedom is given
And taken away at random. My beard grows,
My allotment looks groomed and obedient,
I'm taking to drinking cognac on the patio, smoking
Cigars I can buy anywhere but from a tobacconist.
Somewhere a woman is succumbing to despair,
A man contemplates an empty future,
Children are fractious and uncooperative,
The elderly are isolated at two-arms' length.
I like my space; it's what I always wished for.
A world of my own. A world with a car and a garden,
A community distanced at the end of a phone or laptop,
An unearned income. The sun is shining. Somewhere a person
Dies alone, dies prematurely, dies with little reason.
Who's rolling these dice?
Who's dealing these hands?
'Nothing personal,' they claim,
'It's a matter of accident not design.'
Wrong place, wrong time.

Storm

Storm? What storm?
A little turbulence, a skirmish with a squall.
A punch-up with an unmapped current.
The odd uncharted eddy.

We rode them out with ease; it's a tidy little vessel,
The crew handpicked, well trained, prepared
To traverse new waters.
Of the passengers a few complained, most never noticed.

We have distractions: *Another hand of bridge madam?*
Compliments of the Captain, sir. Enough for most.
Okay, steerage kicked off; they always do.
A few went over, dead of night, unnoticed.

Now we drift blithely under a cloudless sky.
The doldrums so still you can hear a penny drop
From the eyes of a dead man.
The emboldened fish rise to admire our aimlessness.

We've had to manage without First Mate.
Found frothing in the fo'c'sle then
Locked down aft, hallucinating about black clouds
Somewhere over the horizon.

Storm, what storm?
Bring another bottle Bosun.
We could be here for some time.
Let's make the most of it.

'We played 'Loaded' by Primal Scream the other day. It made me think of the lads up North, one lad in particular, a close friend who we lost. I just got a lump in my throat and didn't pull it together in time. When we got back on air I was all choked up.' —*Sara Cox, Ministry Magazine, July 2001*

So I'm leaving Leeds
And over drinks we are making our comparison
Of football teams and their supporters
And I mention Leeds United and Tony Harrison.

Not for the first time
I draw some sharp unknowing jibes
And condescendingly explain
The poet's anger at some '80s mindless soccer scribes.

Harrison's venom split the nation.
Railing at *fuck* daubed in a Leeds graveyard
His work was written off as desecration.
He was never Thatcher's favourite bard.

Then Stephen quietly opened up:
'Graveyards have a tale to tell, there's much to see,
As in my own small town near Glasgow
Whose history can be traced across its tidy cemetery.

Across the back wall lie the older tombs.
You notice all the kids who're under five
Dying from disease and hungry to their bones.
The mammies seldom saw their bairns survive.

And here the paupers' graves grassed over
And there the marble tombs of civic patrons.

In life they were not equal, in death it so remained,
The ones unmarked, the other crafted lavishly by city masons.

And in the corner there the regimented stones.
Memorials to those butchered in the mud of France,
A ritual culling of the cream of Scotland's youth
Who wanted to be heroes but never had a chance.

And here a generation lost to glue and drugs.
Young men, they were my friends, just sixteen years or so.
Don't think I'm joking, I survived through luck.
Why I'm still here I just don't know.

So Mike is 'safe in his Saviour's arms'
With Paddy who's now 'set free'
And here is Sean, 'a loving son',
And the space next to Martin was meant for me.'

We stared in silence at our pints;
Stephen's rep was as a joker.
We'd lurched from Leeds United into life and death.
We hadn't bargained on a choker.

Like a car boot seller who buys without a care
Like a bring-and-buyer who buys more than he brings
So to The Cider House I take my wares
And return overflowing with sustenance and string.
For sustenance I have the milk of human kindness
The bread of heaven and the salt of the earth
And in a mugging of the lame and blind
My bulging pockets of stolen sisal betray my worth.
Tomorrow I'll knit and crochet these pathetic scraps
So important to a man without a lace
And create a piece of second-rate verse
On the back of poets without a face.
And what I leave behind I may think a bargain
But poetry has never helped them through the maze;
Tomorrow as I count my scraps of loot
The cider poets start again and lose themselves in cider-sodden days.
And so to Scottish Jimmy who snores throughout the reading
And equally to gap-toothed Pam
To all you topers with your bloodshot features
I raise a glass; you make me what I am.
We're all doing business down the same old market place
Oh yes we're all exchanging good for bad
But I'm the thief who takes away your memories
That tomorrow you'll not remember that you had.

Today I will write a poem
But first I will make myself some breakfast
The last two slices of a Warburton's Toastie
That has been in the breadbin for over ten days
Begging the question of why they're not mouldy.

Today I will write a poem
But first I will check on my garden
To appraise the night's predations
To chase off the slugs and pull token weeds
Before admiring the cabbages planted by my granddaughter.

Today I will write a poem
But first I will find a screwdriver
And fix that curtain rail
Which has been hanging aslant since last Christmas
And while I am tooled-up secure the loo roll holder.

Today I will write a poem
But first I will take in the news headlines
To remind me of the world's iniquities
To feed my anger and fuel my pen
To celebrate the making of champions.

Today I will write a poem
But first I will do some ironing
How much more disciplined and adult
Not just a daydreaming poet
But a zen master of action and resolve.

Today I will write a poem
Perhaps today it will be a love poem
Not a rant against the imperfect world
I have only ever written love poems when on the verge of madness
And today I feel quite normal.

Yes today I will write a poem
It will sweep and swirl
Laden majestically with classical imagery
Inspired by a week in Paris
In homage to Henry Miller I will call it 'Quiet Days in Cliché'.

Yes tomorrow I will write a poem.

Corralled and hobbled like prairie mustangs,
We pen them in according to their colour, age and size,
Schooling them to break their spirits,
Forcing them to learn new tricks.
They become our servants, docile and less feisty,
Hooves smoothed and harness polished,
But we know deep down
They will always be wild at heart.
They will never truly become what we wish they were.
We have turned them into a cabaret,
A circus of performing words.
Many come to love the limelight,
Can't wait to promenade before a crowd.
But over ninety-nine percent escape our lariats
And roam out there unfettered and unbound,
Visit fleetingly at dead of night
Occasionally crossing our line of vision
Before melting back into the wilderness.
Memories that cannot be roped
Or broken by our wrangler's craft.

Always have your characters
Bite the hand that feeds them
Cut off their noses to spite their face
Judge a book by its cover
Count their chickens before they're hatched
Let the cat out of the bag
Throw the baby out with the bathwater
Then wash their dirty linen in public

Make them
Put the cart before the horse
Look a gift horse in the mouth
Change horses in midstream
Burn their bridges before they come to them
Put all their eggs are in one basket
Then teach their grandmother to suck them
Keep a dog but bark themselves
Shit on their own doorstep
And upset every apple cart
Before washing their dirty linen in public

Insist that they
Always say 'never'
Believe everything they hear
Shoot the messenger
Leave their manners at the door
Rock the boat
Get mad not even
Throw good money after bad

Run before they can walk
Walk before they can crawl
Throw pearls before swine
And always
Always
Always
Wash their dirty linen in public.

So we are looking at a man who's looking at three men whose conversation is intense. Judging by his Hawaiian shirt he's a man who's travelled far or just has an inappropriate dress sense. He makes no pretence at being cool, enigmatic's not his style, he acts the fool.

In his head he's recording every beat of their speech, every fraction of their action, his feat of memory is prodigious. No distractions stall his inner cinecamera. He is the memory babe, the chronicler of a new wave of writers and performers who in part do not wish to be slaves to the prevailing culture of consumption but use their gumption to make a living from their art.

They live on the edge, create their own world, and demand that everyone else takes note. No joke. He takes their lives and weaves and scribes.

It's 1953, they're inside a club and pooling their last dimes. Charlie Parker's playing tonight, he's just been serving time. All the crowd are out tonight, far out but not out of sight. They're there to be seen, to preen, to be out on the town. They're not just following Steppenwolf through that green door, they're busting it down.

'The Subterraneans,' says Ginsberg, 'are hip without being slick, they are intelligent without being corny, they are intellectual as hell and know all about Pound without being pretentious or talking too much about it, they are very quiet, they are very Christlike.' (Did he say that before he met Neal Cassady?) He describes our subject's writing style as 'spontaneous bop prosody'.

The man in the Hawaiian shirt stands out among the grey and black, the zoot suits, shades, and here and there the cropped-hair sandal-wearing girls. He occupies a whorl of shadows, each table candle creates its own tableau along the brick-faced wall. He's having a ball. He's on another plane where something deep inside is dug. He's got the bug. A buzz, a thrum, a wave of energy with each solo, each virtuoso roll of drum. With every number he is reborn, following the cycle of each studied path, each piece leading inexorably to climax, death and a sardonic laugh. In this cave, man he has nothing to lose. In this Theatre of Be-Pop he pays his dues. He may be a drunk and he may act the fool but he is respectful to the bodhisattvas of cool. The other Subterraneans may come and go; Kerouac remains their Caravaggio.

Steal in from the suburb and pull your coat round tight. The sun is disappearing and soon there'll be no light. You're just hoping for a crevice to hide in for the night.

Moonlight floods an avenue, lights up a barren wall. You feel exposed and pause as if waiting for a call. Your senses primed, their radar picking nothing up at all.

Although you're in the shadow the stone has kept its heat. You squat against a canyon wall becoming conscious of a beat. It pulses up into your brain and back down to your feet.

No sound to speak of, just a throb, a flow. An invitation or a warning? Your choice to stay or go.

The locals in these canyons play blindman's hide and seek. Fantasists and predators, the down and out and weak. A fractious bunch of characters who are decadently beat.

It's where they do their business but only after dark. Fugitives and chancers who want to make a mark. It's where they think they won't be found until of course they are.

You put a hand upon the wall, feel the energy inside. It draws you down a cul-de-sac, no place to run or hide. From the blind end of the alley wafts perfume, sweat and fear. A green light seeps into the night through a door that wasn't there.

Your heart is pounding rhythmically in concert with the beat. Your choice to take another step or make a quick retreat. Pushing at the door you hit a wall of heat and a sultry voice says 'Welcome friend, while I find you a seat.'

From Marrakesh to Manchester, Berlin to Bleeker Street, like a string of cool oases lie the ley lines of the beat. Unmarked, unmapped, unplaceable, invisible through day, they lure weary willing seekers to sensual night time play.

The city is a sprawling wen the planners can't defeat; they may control the traffic but they can't control the street. The rhythm of the masses, throbbing hearts a-beat, defeat all jurisdiction; just be careful who you meet.

So if you steal in from the suburb to a city yet unknown, take a walk at midnight when the nighthawks start to roam. And if you come across a green door leading to a cellar, know you're in the footsteps of the wolfman, Harry Haller.

The dance of no going back

It's that dance which says there's no going back
After the preliminaries
After the chitchat and silly jokes
The alcoholic looseners
After the extravagant and out-of-character moves
After the eye contact
The lingering brush of fingers
As you strut your stuff.
You who couldn't dance for toffee
But now it's the thigh-to-thigh touch
Just on the heavy side of light
The clinging shuffle
Hands slipping south.
Yes it's the time of surrender to the backbeat
Like buoys anchored to the seabed, bobbing, swaying
But going nowhere, groin to groin.
A dance where all you want is in your hands
Except that next move
No more dancing away the heartache
No more dancing to the break of dawn
No more dancing until the cows come home
The next dance won't be on this dancefloor
It's the dance of no going back.

Direction of travel

We did not have a map or compass in our hands
The guidebooks lay abandoned on the shelves
As our first moves took us into unfamiliar lands
We relied on instinct and ourselves

The journey so absorbed our concentration
We sweated on without a backward glance
Fumbling onwards to our destination
Not knowing if we'd get a second chance

We ventured blindly but expressing no concern
Through valleys moist with heavenly scented dew
Shuddering together at the point of no return
Slipping into hidden places all anew

It seemed no time since we had first departed
How sweet the sense of ease and satisfaction
And lo we found ourselves exactly where we'd started
Maps and guidebooks had created no distraction

Our journey of discovery had progressed full circle
Relaxed and stilled with momentary meditation
A sideways glance to check the bedside clock
And we were ready to repeat our exploration

Two bottles in
Lying on my back
Willing the movement of the moon
Tracking the passage of satellites
Wishing on the appearance of shooting stars
Capturing the architecture of constellations
Thinking *it's a job and a half*
Being the centre of the universe.
You are lying three foot away.
I sense your heat.
I want to reach across
This infinite space.
To touch you.
In the kitchen she makes coffee.

Shredder

I rediscovered them.

As flat as parchment passed through marble rollers,
A compressed block of captured memory
Triggering those visceral waves of nausea and arousal,
Breaching my sea wall, releasing my monster.

You were always fond of green and purple,
That firm and cursive script, assertive yet so stylish,
Reducing me to adolescent giddiness,
Trembling as I turned each page.

Now they look like some Kesey cut-up,
Surreal streamers of seduction, ribbons of remorse,
Spewing into the present through those mindless blades,
Awaiting reinterpretation from the acid prankster.

Crushing them I smell the aged perfume,
Catapulted to that other world of pain and passion.
Plunging my hands into that fertile litter,
I reap some stupid satisfaction

Each time I change the hamster's bedding.

The art of deception

To look into the eye but not the soul
To grasp the hand firmly but not warmly
To speak with certainty but without feeling
To remember the name but not the face
To act the part but not yourself
To listen intently but not to hear
To agree wholeheartedly but not commit
To say you will and then do not
To flatter idiots but bite your tongue
To walk tall but crawl when not observed
To dish it out but wallow in self-pity
And cry yourself to sleep

Contented in spring

What greater joy (thinks Mr Nagata) than to consider the future
Through a tunnel of pink cherry blossom
The air glacier clear and clean
The pristine snow scarcely melted.

Taking his spring holiday at Blossom Festival
Means sharing beauty with many
A small price but occasionally Mr Nagata finds a seat
And waits for the crowds to thin.

He catches the full sweep of that long-arched path
Soon to be painted with discarded petals.
Later sitting in the bathhouse steaming
Through the gap in a lacquered screen

A warm plum wine at hand
Mr Nagata watches moonlight incite blossom on a single branch
Hears a distant owl wishing him good fortune
And feels ever more uniquely blessed.

Summer pilgrimage

Walking the high road towards Shikoku
Mr Nagata anticipates the next inn
Savours the sweet nectar of cool wine
Feels the soothing fan of a young server.

Mid-summer the dusty road offers no succour
Too old (he thinks) too old
Wishing to turn the clock back ten years
Sweat runs down his neck, salt stings his eyes.

Occasionally fellow travellers offer greetings
Old ways are disappearing
More tyres than shoes on this pilgrimage route
More walking boots than bare feet

In the mountains snow-cold streams and hot springs.
This his twentieth year of pilgrimage
His wife left with children in the city to sweat.
As he clears his mind with prayer and contemplation

The Buddha calls
Fruit ripens on plum trees
Sakura at The House of Sixth Happiness
Has the sweetest breasts.

Falling leaves

Like a character from a Murakami story
Mr Nagata looks through the shutters at the empty street
He takes another sip of his Suntory
He imagines he can hear a beat.

Gone midnight and everything is quiet
Only fallen leaves eddying around the wheels of cars
The young people passed through an hour ago
Birds of Paradise fallen from the stars.

For thirty years he listened to that driving beat
Rising from the cellar club three doors away
He watched the queues stretch down the street
He has heard the masters play.

All things must pass (thinks Mr Nagata philosophically)
Throughout the darkest days the music carried on
People flocked to hear the greatest
Yet now the beat has gone.

He picks an album from the lower shelf
It's one he hasn't heard for years
Stan Getz's *Autumn Leaves*
And allows himself the luxury of tears.

Like a character from a Murakami story
Mr Nagata looks through the shutters at the empty street
He takes another sip of his Suntory
And realises his fingers are tapping to the beat.

In winter

Mr Nagata takes another sip of Ballantyne's
Pulls the burlap sack around his shoulders
Listens to the sigh of shifting sand
Leans back against the sea-smoothed boulders.

Mr Nagata senses voices woven
In the crash of waves, the crack of burning pine
Tomorrow will he slouch off to distant hills
To seek solace in some draughty shrine?

Sheltered from a chilling breeze
He stares into the glowing embers
Surveys the fleeting images
Throws on another log, remembers

The girl he wishes he could forget
Her black hair bobbed, her white neck slender
Sees a music stand, a dextrous hand
Distant memories of an old pretender.

Hums softly thinking of his daughter
Prays for her safety wherever she may be
For his wife he has no such concern
Some far-off stirrings a fading memory.

On the slopes the plum prepares to blossom
Pink bud on the whitest snow
Like the nipples of a comely woman
He knows now is the time to go.

Mr Nagata takes another drink
Heaves himself along the shore
To a wooden shack leaning at a crazy angle
Moonlight streaming through the broken door.

Lighting an incense stick he thanks his gods
Takes the washing line from off the wicker wall
And like a character from a Murakami story
Creates a noose and ends it all.

Prologue

Who goes there
In depth of night?
What terrors lie in store
For a weary foot-sore traveller
Lost upon the moor?

Who sleeps there
On wind-swept slopes?
What shelter can it give?
Relentless and uncompromising,
A barren place to live.

Who works there
On stony ground?
Whose coffers can it fill?
What labour is rewarded
By this sodden Winter Hill?

Spring

This day, spring sunshine turns the dead grass of winter
To a prairie of golden threads.
Days are lengthening, larks are climbing,
Stone walls warming, curlews crying,
Sheep are lambing.

The next day, sky and summit
Are one,
Wrapped in a clinging shroud.
Rain-sodden and sopping,
The bogs absorb then overflow
To scour the drains and gullies,
To fill Scouse kettles from Rivington and Anglezarke.

If dry, lie horizontal.
Look into the blue at the swaying mast.
Try not to feel queasy.
If wet, just marvel at the ingenuity of humankind.

Summer

Cotton grass and ferns hide skeletal walls, disused workings,
Cover farm foundations, abandoned pit shafts, quarried stone,
Disguise the criss-cross of ditches and drains.
Do not be misled.
Do not attempt the shortest route from A to B.
Do not be seduced by the panorama.
Do not think this fine day will be kind to the unprepared.

Observe a silence.
Listen for the muted complaints of carters' horses
Humming in the stones,
Or the songs of tipsy miners from long-abandoned homes.

Beware warm wind, beware the dry spell.
Once is just enough and just too much.
One careless spark, one fag-end,
Incinerates the living, scorches the canvas.
Destroys the balance.

Autumn

An autumn day with lengthening shadow,
Diffused sunbeams that wash not sear,
Days shortening.
It's not New England,
But Old English Rivington dazzles
With reds and golds.

Ancient woodland long gone,
A necklace of new timber
On lower slopes
Frames a harvest moon.

Farmers prepare to bring their beasts down,
Hay stacked high in ancient barns.
Against a venal sunset,
The Pigeon Tower and Pike stand proud:
We will be noticed.

Winter

Crisp winter snow underfoot,
A chilling wind from the East,
A biting squall from the West.
Short days, shallow light.
The ewes shelter on the lower slopes
Where windblown trees provide respite
And give the hungry owl a vantage point.

Wheatear and swallow long gone.
Stoat and weasel holed up.

The tops deserted,
Other than a row of striding skeletons
Silhouetted by a settling sun,
Pulsing silently.

The mast, taut cables straining,
Stays chained to the bedrock.
From all directions on a cloudless winter night,
Its eight rubies on black velvet
Provide a 'welcome back'
To the homebound wanderer.

Epilogue

Mankind must have its way and make its mark.
Yet this fastness cannot be mastered,
Can only be met halfway.
Once these heights were highways
Above the swampy valleys,
Were look-out posts for aliens and enemies,
Carried the stamp of collier and brickworker,
Sustained families immured to all that could be thrown at them.

With four seasons in one day,
Not a place to be ignored.
Not a place to be taken for granted.
A place to be valued, a place for all,
A place to breathe deep and see far,
A place shared,
A place to respect.
A place to take pride in.
Our Winter Hill.

A YEAR ON
THE HILL

A FILM BY
RACHEL APPLETON

WRITTEN & PRODUCED BY DAVE MORGAN · MUSIC BY KEVIN BATES
NARRATED BY STELLA BLACKBURN & DAVE MORGAN

AUDIO PRODUCTION BY JOHN MAYCRAFT AT SOUND CAFÉ · PHOTO BY JULIA UTTLEY · DESIGN BY FLAPJACK PRESS
COPYRIGHT © 3SP PRODUCTIONS 2022

Bolton International
Film Festival

At The Taste of Greece Maria smiles a welcome and takes my order and Stergos, with his deepening sense of English humour, sardonically says how much he is enjoying the Bolton summer and I launch into my theory that August is God's way of reminding parents that hell doesn't have to be hot and that we English get used to having summer in April and October, when Sabina pipes in from behind the counter, 'But think of all the beautiful things about your English summer,' and I dismissively say, 'When you've thought of a few let me know,' and she comes straight back and says, 'Clouds, so many clouds of so many kinds in the course of an hour; the rain, so many different types of rain even in one day; and the gardens, the thirty shades of green, the trees,' so I give in and count my blessings and eat my yeeros, watching orange-toned women tottering out of the side-door of The Swan to the strain of 'Pretty Woman' murdered by some would-be Roy Orbison, high-heels skidding on rain-soaked flag-stones, handbags on heads, and the truth is that in this very August moment I'd much prefer to be in clear-skied, olive-treed and arid Greece.

When I heard the learned laureate

The Poet Laureate reads his commemorative poem on the 200th anniversary of the founding of the Royal Astronomical Society, January 2020 – with apologies to Walt Whitman's 'When I Heard the Learn'd Astronomer'.

When I heard the learned laureate,
How quickly my mind was flooded
With my own celestial memories.
I didn't really believe in stars until I was sixteen.
They were in the books and songs
But seldom in our soot-filled sky.
The sun and moon yes, we had fleeting evidence of both;
Our goldfish gulping round its overheated global world in summer,
My sister forecasting Martian invaders
When the moon looked closer or bigger or redder.
If it was light we were out but not the stars,
If dark we were in behind drawn curtains
Safe from prying neighbours.
Released from childhood,
Walking the night streets after seeing a girlfriend home,
I spotted them:
Flickering pricks of stellar light through the smoke-ravaged sky.
But no shape or pattern, nothing like *The Sky at Night*.
Where were those other celestial entities of *Journey into Space*,
Their fiery reds and seductive greens?
At nineteen I lay on a grassy headland facing the Bristol Channel,
Freed from the city, lost in an inky blackness,
Intense and deep, and there…
Yes, a celestial pulsing net punching out signals
In interstellar morse code.

So this was it, I thought, until my friend,
Forcing my gaze to three stars in line, announced
'Orion's Belt,' then 'The Plough,' and 'There, the North Star.'
I had my epiphany. I felt greater for it; a oneness with it all.
I felt less for it. Dust, just stardust.

Doomed infatuation

It is ten days now of hard frost,
Only the slightest hint of snow and little cloud.
Each sunny day extends and draws a little life;
From cold-baked cracks in frozen soil
Somehow the simple snowdrops force their way.
And the handsome jay flies closer by the day.

I break the ice on shallow pond,
Afraid the frogs will cease to breathe.
I put out bread and scatter seeds
To meet my regular visitor needs.
It feels as though the frost is here to stay.
And daily closer comes the handsome jay.

A major domo of a wood pigeon,
Two perfectly presented collared doves,
Tumbling troupes and foraging flocks.
The large, the small, the bold and meek,
Queue up and through the offerings pick their way.
But there within the evergreen observes the handsome jay.

We now had twenty days of hard frost,
The town transformed by winter sun.
I peer more often through my kitchen window
Waiting for my prince to come.
I hope the frost will deepen and never go away.
To see my gifts rewarded by the presence of the jay.

My dreams are melting with the rain,
The frost has slipped away,
And leaving just a memory
So has the handsome jay.

'The trouble with fossils,' says Sam,
'Is that they just look like rocks.'
The past and present fused
In this disused quarry high above the reservoir.

Towering rock faces
Slow-weathered by nature,
Ripped apart for civic progress,
Now lie neatly stacked like toy blocks.

Those steam hammer generals
With their masonic secrets
Knew their geology well enough
To keep the cities proud and solid.

Now swallows wheel above
The heather rich in honey bee,
And all is silent, save the subliminal morse
Of fossils singing from within the stone.

Old track

A deep-driven carter's track
Between two high walls of well-dressed stone.
No farmer's labours these,
Coiling around cones of splintered shale
Now purple with advancing heather.

Shaped from nature by a mason's hand,
Blackened by the fall-out of valley towns
And softened by a century of moorland ingress,
The mossy walls have stood the ravages of time
And offered refuge to the weasel and the wheatear.

The men who laboured here are long since gone,
The quarry long since silent,
But track and wall remain their testimonial.
Somewhere a carter's cry is carried on the wind
And the mute complaints of horses are captured in the stone.

I love to wander
                    towards the light
              without a plan
                          no end in sight
              without a goal
                              no rush just stroll
                    harmless lazy walking
                                    where my senses do the talking

                              Hear

the sound of silent footsteps

                              See

the imprint form, then disappear

                                  Taste

the space I am creating

                                  Touch

the air I am displacing

                                      Smell

the scent of sweet surprise

                                        Open

my eyes and

                    Breathe

A wanderful mind will go, will go where it will go.
Mindful and merciful.
Never mind, always mind, just let it wander.

So you're sitting on that outcrop looking down the valley through the man-made forest and just catching a glimpse of the lake through the trees and it's a big sky, all as you imagined and no-one comes on this track which is mainly overgrown and you've been treading whinberries for twenty minutes and in no way is this isolation, you're only two miles from an A-road and on a day like this it doesn't feel like desolation, it's not quite approaching dark and there's no fear of puma or bear, although beware the midges, they can eat you alive; a short way to the East is the city and its satellites, and in that metropolis of a million there are people who are more isolated, more desolate, more threatened, and you marvel at your luck and take credit for your initiative in hiking from that bus stop on that A-road, when you suddenly become aware of someone beside you and it's not frightening, but it's about to become chastening as Gary says, 'That's your trouble friend, overthinking; you're polluting the best of the day with your idle thoughts when all you have to do is let go, soak yourself in the clean air; if there are no lilies at least consider the heather, breathe it in, become part of it, put your rational thoughts aside for just ten minutes… just ten minutes, they'll still be there to chew you up later, no point of making this small journey to ruin it with thinking,' and the sun is setting behind you, and an orange glow suffuses that little snatch of lake, and a pale crescent moon, scarcely visible, appears above the city in the East, and the air is warm and still, and the midges are enjoying their supper, but it doesn't matter until tomorrow.

Bravado

Do not presume to tell me how to age
I'll do what I can do to stay his hand
Put porridge in the hour glass to replace the sand
Do not attempt to put me in a cage

Do not pretend that life is more than just *a bowl of ferrets* *
I'll do what I can do to duck death's icy gaze
Wear shades and scuttle in the undergrowth
Do not presume to tell me how to age

Do not insist the master jester of this absurd universe
Has any purpose other than mere malice
That he thinks more of the stable than the palace
Do not insult me with your fairytales or worse

Do not attempt to lock me in your shed
From hereon in the dice man's calling all the shots
Bring out the booze, the fat cigar, the pot
Let me sparkle, let me burn; tomorrow is light years ahead

* A phrase from the poem 'One for Sorrow, Yootha Joyce' by Hovis Presley
(*Poetic Off Licence*, Flapjack Press).

Acknowledgements

Versions of several poems have been published previously or been commissioned for specific events. These include:

'A life of biblical proportions' (*Milestones Poetry Competition Anthology* [Milestones Society & Write Out Loud]).

Quiet days in Cliché' (*Best of Manchester Poets, Vol. 3* [Puppywolf]).

'We try to capture memories' (*Warrington Collegiate Writers, Vol. 1*).

'Old track' (*Littoral Magazine*).

'Round Barn Quarry' (*Earth Love Magazine*).

'The Subterraneans', 'Mr Nagata: Falling leaves' & 'Steppenwolf: This is the city' (Beat is Back at Marsden Jazz Festival, the latter also in *Whitman on Walls* [Compagnia de' Colombari]).

'Mr Nagata: Summer pilgrimage' (*Poetry Bay Magazine*).

'A year on the hill' (Right to Roam 125th anniversary march on Winter Hill, subsequently animated for the Bolton International Film Festival by Rachel Appleton with music by Kevin Bates).

'Direction of travel', 'Shredder' & 'Doomed infatuation' (*Wood Street Writers Anthology* [Preeta Press]).

'Bravado' (*The Anthology of Tomorrow* [Flapjack Press]).

flapjackpress.co.uk